Dedicated to my beautiful mother
Angela Wilkins
July 19th 1960- August 28th 2016
I just want to make you proud of me

I Love You and Miss You!

Table of Contents

Preface

This book is for EVERYBODY! This is for the kid from Iowa that lives on the farm that doesn't have a trainer. The one whose dad never played sports. The one on youtube everyday watching the top players in the country work with their trainer wishing they had one. This is for the dad whose kid loves the sport but played a different sport. This is for the kid who has a trainer that doesn't have a clue. Or the kid who comes from a football town but only likes basketball.

Everybody can learn from this. From those stated above to the top 100 kids. Not just point guards but all players. This is the time to develop point guard characteristics seeing as the game is going positionless. I don't know it all but I know a lot. I'm a visionary, an innovator, and a creator. I look at things differently and in depth. So I see all the little details that separate the good from the great.

This is the reason for this book. As the position evolves, it takes a lot more to actually be good let alone great. Your older influences are probably telling you you're good if you're the prototypical guard from their era, but, I'm here to tell you what a Point Guard is in this era. I'm not writing this to tell you how to be good. I'm writing this to inspire the greatest point guard of all time.

To do so, I have to first let you know the types of point guards and the history of the position. Then inform you on what the perfect point guard is. Then I'll tell you how to do it. Then wait to hear about you years down the line and hope it's because you read this book, not once but once a month! I'm at the perfect age to do so. I'm young enough to relate to the younger generations yet old enough to relate to the older generations.

Chapter 1
The Evolution Of The PG

Point guard (PG), by definition, is a simple concept, the backcourt player who directs the offense. Now we all know it's nowhere near that simple and if you don't know that, maybe because you're too young. You'll soon realize within the next few paragraphs.

The PG directs the offense, yes, but the PG also is the leader who gets on his teammates when they can do better. They also motivate and encourage a teammate when their confidence is down. The PG is the coach on the floor. The PG is responsible for carrying out the game plan the coaching staff puts together. In the words of the legendary Isiah Thomas,

"My job was to take it off the blackboard and make it come to life on the floor."

With that quote, along with the evolution of the position, the point guard needs to be re-explained. Your dad, grandfather, uncles, and coaches probably tell you that today's PG's are not "real" PG's. Well they're right........and wrong!

Old School 80's PG's: Why they're RIGHT!

When talking about the point guard position the two most notable names of the 80's are Magic Johnson and Isiah Thomas. Both considered Top 5 of all time and rightfully so. In the last 3 decades, only 3 times has a team won a championship with the PG leading the team in scoring and assists and these 2 guys led 2 of those teams. The other one, well, we'll get to him later.

Let's start with Isiah Thomas (drafted in 1981), listed as 6'1. He's what the oldheads consider a "real" point guard. Small, quick, floor general that ran the team and scored when his team needed it. In this era, there were more PG's like Isiah than there were like Magic Johnson. In fact, the majority of the PG's in the league were at the time.

John Stockton was the other "All-Time Great" in the same mold as Isiah. Less of a scorer than Isiah but could score well in his own right. Stockton didn't look to score but could shoot from wherever which opened up the floor for his penetration. Stockton was one of the PG's that made the Pick & Roll a necessity in every offense in the NBA today. He was one of the greatest of all time in that regard.

Magic however (drafted in 1979) is what Jay-Z calls,

"A 1 of 1, that means none before it none to come."

He definitely was, but only in that era. The reason most oldheads consider Magic the best ever is because he was like all the prototypical point guards in that era, pass first and score when needed. The big difference was the fact that Magic was 6'9. He mastered running the offense by putting smaller defenders on his hip.

At that time, he was a "freak of nature" at that position. Which he was but just like anything else that can be considered great at the time of its existence, evolution happens. Evolution makes you look back at that great thing and realize that that was just the starting point. There is always going to be somebody thinking...

"What if THAT could also do THIS? And THIS? And THAT?"

90's PG's: Why They're Wrong

Evolution is:
"The gradual development of something, especially from a simple to a more complex form."
I was born in 86' but in 1988 one of my favorite and most underrated PG's of all time was drafted, Rod Strickland. Rod was the prototypical New York City PG. He couldn't shoot it that good but could still get anywhere he wanted on the floor. Besides having a crazy handle Rod was one of the best finishers at the PG position. It makes a lot of sense that he's the Godfather of possibly the best finishing PG of all time, but we'll get to that later.

Let's go back to Magic, we talked about his strengths which he mastered like nobody else, now let's explore his weaknesses. At 6'9 playing the point he was a "freak of nature" then but now, not so much because he wasn't very athletic. Didn't dunk on people and couldn't blow by guys with similar size and athleticism which we first realized when the Bulls put Scottie Pippen on him. He couldn't hit the 3 off the dribble but could in the form of a set shot.

Putting Magic in this era would prove where he fits in this process of evolution. He started it. Not to discredit anything he ever did nor discredit his spot in the top 5 of PG's which never changed and never will. His IQ & Leadership was his mastery. He was and is still the best ever at running a team, in my opinion of course. I'm just stating that skill set wise he's not close to what he inspired for the next few decades.

So, I'm saying that because of him we have what we see today, the "Big Guard." All evolution has a forefather that needs to be appreciated more than those that transcend it. For example, the Wright Brothers invented the first successful airplane. What they invented is nothing even close to the airplanes we have today. We have private jets today.
Bill Lear the inventor of the Private Jet wasn't trying to make a better version of the original airplane the Wright Brothers created. He was trying to make a better version of a military jet. As evolution goes on the newest innovators are trying to "one up" the innovators before them not the original inventor. Therefore, the inventors' invention gets more and more forgotten about and downplayed when it shouldn't. So, due to that I would like to say,

Thank You, Magic, The Forefather of the "Big Guard."
From me and this younger generation who love the PG's that you inspired without knowing where the process of evolution begin.

In 1991 Magic retired due to finding out he was HIV Positive. He won 5 NBA Championships. By this time, the evolution was already in play. In 1990 Gary "The Glove" Payton entered the league. He was a 6'4 version of Magic. Game almost identical and could be Magic Johnson's basketball son. The only difference with the glove was that he wasn't the "humble" type. He was the cocky, get in your face, and talk trash type.

Like Magic he was a natural leader with a high IQ. The Glove wasn't the most athletic but could lock up smaller guards or bigger wings. He could post up, score, and facilitate at a high level. What everybody remembers about him is that he would tell you about it the whole time he was doing all of the above.

The next step in the evolution of bigger guard came the form of my favorite player of all time and the reason I love the game, Penny Hardaway. When Magic retired Penny was a freshman in college. Drafted in 1994 Penny was a 6'7 PG. He had the same tools as Magic and The Glove. However, wasn't a master in IQ and leadership like Magic and the Glove was but not many were. He was smart and leadership wise he led his team but he wasn't an Alpha Dog. He was a Beta Dog that became an Alpha Dog when his team needed it.

What made him the next step in the evolution of the "Big Guard" was athleticism, shooting off the dribble, and ball handling. Penny's handle was so good he didn't have to put smaller guards on his hip. He could face up and smaller defenders couldn't stay in front of him. When he played against a Michael Jordan or a Scottie Pippen they had trouble guarding him because he was their size and athletic but had a handle like a small guard. He was a matchup nightmare for anybody. In my opinion if Penny didn't have injury problems he could've been a top 3 PG of all time in my and other's opinion.

In 1994 a 6'4, super-fast, high IQ, rebounding, super distributing, lockdown defender named Jason Kidd. These descriptions make sense considering he has 118 career Triple Doubles (More than any other PG I remember with my own 2 eyes). Kidd had good guidance coming up in Oakland. It's noted that he's learned a lot from Gary Payton and his Father. Kidd was like a faster Gary Payton but with John Stockton's facilitating. He effected the game in every way possible. He was the first Big & Fast PG.

One of the next phases in the evolution of the Point Guard was drafted in 1996. A 6 foot on paper but 5'11 in real life, Allen Iverson. "The Answer" "AI" or whatever you want to call him. The reason 3 is the most popular jersey number in basketball. The smallest player ever to average 30 ppg in a season. What's even crazier is he did it 3x. He wasn't the first "Scoring PG" but he was the best "Scoring PG" ever. Super quick, super athletic, tough as nails with a killer instinct and his crossover was the most popular signature move of all-time. He used this move to embarrass the greatest player of all time in his prime. I could talk about AI for 3 chapters but just to sum it up, every PG in the NBA that came in the League after him was at least influenced by him if he wasn't there favorite player of all time.

In the same draft as AI you had Stephon Marbury, the prototypical New York City Point Guard. Flashy, tough minded, playground style PG that even if he wasn't your favorite player you loved watching him. Also in the historical '96 draft you had back to back MVP Steve Nash. Nash was an elite distributor and shooter. Often compared to John Stockton that's who his game is most like offensively but he's noted as saying Isiah Thomas is his favorite PG.

In '98 the possibly flashiest point guard of all time was drafted. White Chocolate, formally known as Jason Williams. At one point people, would say White Chocolate couldn't do anything simply. Everything had a flare to it. The handle was on a 100 the vision was just about the same. This is somebody who did a behind the back pass off of his elbow. It was impossible not to watch him if he was on TV. You just never knew what he was going to do. To his credit, he started the Steph Curry jumper, when you pull a long 3 and don't hold your follow through. Believe me he had everybody adding flash to their game at the time.

The next 2 in this evolution was the start of what you see today. Or at least what GM's and coaches around the league look for every year when draft time comes around. The "big and athletic" scoring guard with handle like a small guard started in the 1999 Draft with Steve "Franchise" Francis and Baron Davis. These 2 had the ability to make you fall on the perimeter then finish with contact on the big or flat out dunk on them... not to mention they can shoot with range.

Remember when I talked about your elders saying you're not a real point guard if you didn't play the position like the point guards from their era? Well these two is probably when they first started saying this. They probably followed that statement with, "He's a 2 guard in a Point Guard's body." Because these dudes seemed like score first guards people undervalued their ability to distribute the ball. They were point guards they just had swingman attributes.

With the last 2 in the evolution along with this next one I believe the 2 best Point Guards along with another in the top 5 in the NBA today have directly morphed from. So, this is the end of the discussion on the old era, in today's terms. The next guy was drafted in 2001. Took a couple years to fit in the NBA but once he did he went on a tear around the league.
Famously known for trying to put up 100,000 shots in in 73 days before his doctor told him to slow down because he would injure his shoulder.

We talked about Point Guards who used their jumper to open up their game to make plays for other, well Gilbert Arenas used his jumper kill whoever was on him. In his best season, he averaged 29.1 PPG. To sum it up his nickname was "Hibachi the guy who started shooting 3's and walking down court before it drops. The difference is he had the balls to do it for the game winner. I haven't seen many point guards as confident as him.

New Age & Who They Remind You Of

The "Greatest Era of Point Guards" is now. Nobody disagrees, not even the Greats from the past. The reason for that is today's guards borrow from multiple guys back in the day. But not just the Point Guards, they borrow from wings and bigs. They have more in their game. Now they have a fade away in their game. They finish like wings. They have step backs in their game. Point Guards today think they can do everything and work on everything.

They clearly didn't listen to their elders that tried to keep them inside the box.

DISCLAIMER: I am not saying that they are a better version than those that they are reminiscent of just saying they borrowed parts of their game from them or just so happen to play like them.

- Deron Williams is directly cut from the cloth of Gary Payton and Jason Kidd with a better jump shot.

- Chris Paul is mixture between Isiah Thomas and John Stockton.

- Rajon Rondo reminds me of Steve Nash and John Stockton with a little bit of Gary Payton defensively.

- Kyle Lowry is a "Philly Point Guard" with the toughness he brings to the game. But he also has Gary Payton and Kidd with his ability to affect almost every stat in the box score.

- Derrick Rose was the first of the super athletic new age guard. To me he's a mixture of Baron Davis, Stephon Marbury and Rod Strickland with how he finishes at the rim.

- Russell Westbrook is just something different. Him and Rose were drafted the same year but all the talk was about Rose. They would say Westbrook is athletic also but we don't know if he'll really be able to make the transition to a Point Guard. If you questioned that you were wrong. Even if injuries didn't effect D Rose's career I still don't believe he would've still been better than Russell like he was in the earlier years of their careers. Westbrook is like

Kidd in how he affects every stat in the stat sheet and gets up the court in no time. He brings the same attitude as an Allen Iverson and Gary Payton. Kobe Bryant loves Russell's mentality and that's because killers respect killers. He's also a mixture of Steve Francis and Baron Davis and at only 6'3 he is the best rebounding guard of all time. Right now he is averaging a triple double right now. Right now he is the gold standard for Point Guards. He is first in scoring with 30 a game, top 3 in assists, and 10th in rebounding behind all big men. After this season all scouts will be looking for guards who can potentially average a triple double. Russ is changing the league.

- In the last chapter I told you that only 3 teams have won the championship with their point guard leading in scoring and assist. The first two were Magic Johnson and Isiah Thomas and the 3rd is Steph Curry. Steph for a 3-year stretch was everybody's favorite Point Guard and that's because people think they never seen anything like him but we have. It's just a mixture of two different guys. He shoots it Gilbert Arenas in the sense of he doesn't miss and he wants to kill you with it. His shot selection is terrible. Terrible for everybody else except him. You have to deny him and play him tight because he needs next to no space or time to get a shot off. But when you play up you risk the chance of getting crossed. His handle reminds me of Steve Nash more than anybody. It's crafty and deceptive not meant to break you down but just to get to what he really wants to do.

- John Wall is one of the more underrated guys in the league. Year after year he is top 3 in assist while averaging around 20 points. All the while never being mentioned in top 5 categories. This year he is being mentioned as he should. What makes him different though is style. He is one of the only guys in the league that doesn't really remind you of anybody in the past. His end to end speed with the ball may remind you of J Kidd but He's faster. Handle wise he doesn't have the most exciting handle. His speed is what gets him in the paint. He has a handle like Deron Williams, he'll catch with a crossover but he's not really trying to it's just to get where he's trying to go. Athletically he is up there with any other point guard you can name but since he's been in the league he has simplified his game. You rarely see him dunk. I think Sam Cassell being one of his coaches when he got in the league is the reason his game is simplified and to the point but all in all he's in my top 5.

- Kyrie Irving, every kid's favorite. I'll say this one time and after that you'll never hear me say it again, BEST HANDLE OF ALL TIME, CLEARLY, NO DEBATING, GOES TO KYRIE IRVING. Because of this, people actually think he's a point guard, he is NOT. He is like Allen Iverson and Jamal Crawford. Built like point guards, handle like point guards, but the mentality of a shooting guard. They are shot creators. Kyrie is also one of the best finishers ever and best shooters of the bounce ever. So here is a question for you, if you had all of these attributes why would you pass? In all seriousness he has never really had to and the Cavs know it that's why LeBron plays the point. So now you might be asking, why are you bringing him up if he's not a point guard? Because he has attributes that any guard should strive for. In the next ten years guards no matter the size will have to be shot creators and crafty finishers. I'll give you a great example, Isiah Thomas of the Boston Celtics. These 2 are pretty much the same player different sizes though. Isaiah is 5'9 and averaging 29.2 ppg because he can finish very well and create shots off the bounce.

- Damian Lillard is my favorite point guard behind Russell Westbrook. The reason is, he is point guard who truly understands his strengths, shooting. Not only does he understand his strength he knows how to use his strength to maximize everything else in his game and make his teammates better. He plays off of his 3 point shot because simply put, you can't leave him open, at all. If he uses a ball screen you have to chase him over top which puts him in a position to be a playmaker. He thinks shoot first. If they take that away get to the rim. If there is no help shoot. If help steps up pass to whoever they're guarding. Sounds too simple right? It actually is. The game is about making the defense pick their own poison and Dame is one of the best at it. Also can't forget to say this, study his 1 dribble and 2 dribble pull up. Watch how hard and low he dribbles before coming into his shot and how quickly he gets his feet set.

- There are 3 guys who are not traditional point guards by body type and have actually played other positions before converting but i have to bring them up even though I won't go into detail. LeBron James (of course), James Harden, and Giannis

Antetokounmpo. These are the guys that are going to make the league almost impossible to get into because the body type they bring to the position. Now GM's are going to be looking for that. Like i said about evolution, you just need to see something out of the ordinary and then ask yourself, "What if that could do this and this and that?" That's what they are and I won't go into detail because I will in the next book.

Chapter 2
What it takes to be a Point God

Leader/Communicator

Hands down, the most important attribute. No one attribute can singlehandedly keep you in a game like being a true leader and communicator. Leaders show their team how hard you should be playing, what spots you should be in, picking teammates up when they're down, and getting on them when they're not playing up to their potential. Sound familiar? Yeah it sounds like a "Coach on the floor." The term often used to describe what a point guard is.

If you're a great communicator, you're team we'll be prepared every play of the game because you're calling out the plays on both sides of the floor and keeping them focused. This cuts about 5 to 6 mistakes out of each game. College coaches drool over talented players who are leaders. This is also one of the attributes that's hard to obtain. Some people just have it already. If you are the best player or leading scorers on your you are leader without even knowing. I've had point guards that didn't understand that the team looks to them for leadership by default. If this is you understand this and work on this unexpected responsibility you have.

Mental Toughness

Mental toughness is the ability to battle through situations such as bad calls from the refs or your team being down 8 with 2 minutes left and still believing you can win. I know this to be very true. In college, we had a game where we were down by 29 at the half and won by 10. I know about battling through. Mental toughness is also having a bad game but in the final moments you still have the confidence to finish strong and come up with big plays. Your shot is not falling but you still find other ways to help your team. That could be rebounding, defense, or setting teammates up.

Mental toughness is, no matter how the game is going you still have your eyes set on winning. Fearlessness is another word for it. You need to go into any situation with no fear, feeling like teams have to get through you to get a win. Everybody doesn't have it and those who don't, unless being coached the right way, may never develop it.

Different Components of IQ

1. Controlling Tempo

Controlling tempo can make you a good point guard. Some point guards may not be able to shoot, may not be a great passer, may not be able to finish that well, but they can control the tempo of the game. If your opponent is an up-tempo team and you make sure your team gets back on defense and slow it down and get your team into sets, then you become that team's biggest problem. Not the leading scorer on your team. If the they slow it up, you make sure you put pressure on them to speed them up you are the biggest problem. If you push the ball make or miss, then you are the biggest problem.

You should at any point in the game be able to remember the last 3 possessions. The reason being, if a team scores a few quick baskets and you slow it down then you are controlling the tempo. If you, upon catching an outlet pass, turn, look, and can take a screenshot of the floor and see your transition break numbers in a split second (surveying the floor to see if you have a 3 on 2, 2 on1, 4 on 3 etc.), then you are controlling tempo. This allows you to know whether to push it or slow it down and get into a set.

On another note, there are other ways to control tempo. For example, If you see something that can be exploited, DO NOT be afraid to tell your coach. This could be a specific mismatch, certain play the other team has trouble guarding, or a simple pick and roll that has been working the last few possessions. Plenty of times my coach called something and I said, 'Nah coach we going with this, I see something.' This is the mark of true floor general. Running the same thing that works multiple times in a row can take a point spread from 7 to 15. Then a timeout is called because there is too much momentum. Like the saying goes, "If it ain't broke, don't fix it."

2. Knowing Personnel

This is what is not taught enough. Most coaches preach 'pass to the open man' when they should be saying 'pass to the open man, depending on who it is and where they're at on the floor.' Some players are open because it's part of the game plan. You as a point guard need to know your team better than anybody else. You need to know their strengths, weaknesses, hot spots, as well as when they are not engaged. This is part of being a coach on the floor.

In college, I had a few bigs that teams felt they never had to worry about. Because of this the hedge man would sag to keep me from getting to the rim. I used this against teams. I would come off the screen and pull up around the foul line since there would be no real help. On the shot, it would be a late contest and if I missed then my screener would be in position to get an offensive rebound. Because I knew my personnel I could take what the other coach thought was a disadvantage and make it an advantage.

We also had 2 players that you could consider our sixth man. They were two of the streakiest players I've ever seen in my life. As soon as they came in, I made sure they got touches because if they were on, they were a momentum swing waiting to happen. Plenty of times they took us from a from up two to a double-digit lead and forced coaches to call timeouts.

We also had another player who was a starter and was our utility/glue guy. He wasn't much of a shooter, but he rebounded on both sides of the floor, was very good in transition, and was nearly unstoppable on the baseline. Because of this, I always looked for him ahead in transition and on the baseline in the half court.

Our lockdown defender had a nice mid range so I used to hype him up to get to his spots and pull up. He was 6'4, long, super athletic, with a high release. So sometimes it was just a matter of letting him know nobody was going to block his shot. This gave him confidence. Him being as athletic as he was if I could get him the ball in transition I did. I tried to get him dunks because if i did that we would get momentum. You can always use momentum. Plus defensively he did a lot for us. You got to make sure he's rewarded for that.

My man who I went to high school with was playing the 5 for us. We were playing small ball before it was popular lol. Because of this he always had mismatches. He was really a wing but rebounded like a big. I used to always give him the ball in the high post because he could shoot and his first step was probably the quickest on the team so they couldn't guard him there.

Our last starter was my roommate who also was a good defender and after our first couple years became a good shooter. I always looked to get him open shots and if he hit one I made sure he got another one the next play. Funny part is if you ask him he would tell you I looked him off lol. If you reading this you know that wasn't the truth, you was greedy fam (lol).

Knowing everybody's strengths made the game easy for everybody. That championship season had a flow to it. In the league playoffs we won every game by at least 17. We were just clicking on all cylinders. In the chip game I just focused on steering the ship. I had 16 but it was a back breaking 16 that came whenever they were trying to get momentum. I used the right tools in the right situation to build the perfect house.

Jumper/Floater

If you can't shoot or hit a floater then every other skill you have drops a level. This is what opens up your game. As a point guard, you don't have to have a great jump shot or floater, but, it has to be good enough for the defense to have to get up on you. If your strengths are penetrating and kicking/finishing but you can't hit a mid-range jumper or a floater well enough, then your strengths aren't as strong. That's because the defense will sag off which makes it hard to penetrate.

If your floater is sub-par, then the help defense will let you shoot it all day. A floater makes help defenders contest, which opens up the dump off pass. This keeps shot blockers guessing and that is always good. Remember this, big men are less effective when they have to think. Avoid having this on your scouting report,

"Go under ball screens and stay home and give a late contest when he gets in the lane."

This means you're not that much of a threat and have some work to do. That should be your goal. The one good thing I can say about your shot being your weakness, it's the easiest to fix.

Vision

This one thing EVERY point guard must have, vision. If you as a point guard are an extension of the coach on the floor, then you should be able to see everything on the floor. This starts and ends with ball handling. You should be able to dribble while keeping your head up which may be difficult under pressure defense circumstances but it is a MUST HAVE. The elite passers have the vision to see a pass develop and throw it before the receiver even knows their open while being guarded.

Vision even goes as deep as constantly surveying the floor in situations such as receiving the ball. Most elite passers are surveying the floor right before the ball hits their hands. This allows the touch pass that we all like when we see but never realize only high assist guys make. One trick I can give you to start practicing in pickup games,

"See but never stare."

Meaning when surveying the floor never lock your eyes on anything. When you see something developing keep your head on a swivel as if you didn't see it. Youtube the best passers and you'll see what i'm talking about.

Ball Handling

In today's game, it's, Kyrie, Steph, or Mal Crawford, when you ask, "Who has the best handle?" For me it's Kyrie easily because he stays the lowest, is the best at ball protection, best in traffic, and has the best east west game. But realistically, I don't even know how it would be possible to get your handle like that. But if you work to get to that level then imagine how good your handle would be. Let me put it like this your handle is your car. It gets you where you want to go.

Some cars are just faster, transition from gear to gear better, handle turns at high speeds better, handle tough road conditions better, and maneuver through traffic better. While others can't handle tough road conditions, crash when they go to fast, and shoot their transmission when they take off to fast. I'm sure by now you get what I'm saying. Do what you got to do to get upgrade to a Ferrari. Study the great handlers and practice the moves!

*Video suggestions on where and how to study in "Add-On Bundle"
The other aspect to ball handling is handling pressure. Being able to get where you want while getting pressured or being able to handle pressure while waiting for the play to develop. You may be waiting for a big to get good position on the block, waiting for a shooter to come off a stagger, or waiting for a big to come set a screen for you. No matter what you maybe waiting for you better be able to seal your man off and create separation to let the play develop because being a point guard means it's not always about you. You have to go with the clear mismatch sometimes and play off of that.

Pace (Change of Speeds)

Pace is a special thing to see in a young player. As rare as Gerald green's athleticism, but every time you see it you're stuck just watching it. John Wall maybe the fastest guard in the league but would he be an all-star without understanding pace? NO WAY! When you play at one speed you're easy to guard no matter how fast you are. When you can switch it up the defense is now on their heels guessing and at your mercy. Andre Miller wasn't even close to being one of the fastest guards in the NBA but he managed to be in the league for 12+ years due to

Pace on top of IQ. He's not fast but his change of speeds allows him to get past players who are quicker than him.

Pick & Roll/Pop

The ball screen is a big deal in the NBA and College. EVERY team uses them. If played well it can create easy scoring opportunities all game. The good guards can come off the ball screen draw the hedge man and hit the roll or pop guy. The elite guards can come off and read the help stepping up on the roll or pop guy and hit their man. Mastering the pick and roll can get you into and keep you in the league. The most important thing is being able to shoot behind the screen if your defender goes under. If you can't consistently knock that down, YOU ARE NOT A THREAT IN THE PICK & ROLL.

As a coach, I'm telling my hedge man to sag to protect the pass to the roll man and have my guard go under. There will be no options for you once you come off. My guys in the corner don't have to step over to help on the roll man. If you can't shoot behind the screen you have 2 options at the most that are easy to guard but if you can there are 7 options that can be exploited ALL GAME. I will further explain those options in my "Advanced Basics Training Guide" eBook. Study Chris Paul and Steve Nash they'll show you everything you need to know about the pick & roll.

Finishing

Finishing is something that wasn't much of a necessity in the NBA just a decade ago for PG's. It was a bonus that sometimes set you apart from other point guards. Due to

the evolution of the point guard position, you may not even make the league if you can't finish. A coach's nightmare is a point guard that can get in the lane, finish, and draw fouls. Kyrie is 6'2 and not one of the most explosive guys vertically but is easily one of the best finishers.
PRACTICE ALL TYPES OF FINISHES. Off foot, high glass, reverse, double clutch, hang and release on the way down, as well as through contact finishes. But it's not just what he does in the air it's his setup also. He's great at creating an angle to get the shot off before he takes off. Kyrie and James Harden are the best at setting up the finish. That's who you should study.

Chapter 3
How to Develop

Development is hands down the most important thing, yet the most overlooked thing when trying to be successful in any sport. Rankings supersede everything to most kids, parents, or handlers of kids. People look for the shortcut to being ranked rather than the gradual track to being great. Excuse the bad grammar I'm about to use but,

"IT AINT AND I REPEAT IT AINT NO SHORTCUT TO BEING GREAT."

They look to get on a sponsored (Nike, Under Armour, or Adidas) AAU team. As well as a big time high school, all the while keeping their same mediocre work ethic. Let me tell you the truth, if you figure out weaknesses and continuously develop those weaknesses and you're not athletic but athletic enough and puberty is on your side before your last year of AAU, you will eventually be ranked. The oldheads used to say, "If you're good enough they'll find you." True, politics willing.

There are two sides of development, Physical and Mental. The physical is the first thing scouts at all levels look at first. It seems that they believe if you have the size and athleticism then skill can be taught. I somewhat disagree but I'm not a "professional" scout and that's another story for another day. I believe that if somebody has a high IQ and skill level then size and athleticism doesn't matter as much but if somebody has high level athleticism and low IQ and Skill there's not much you can do with them.

For example, whenever a little guard kills in college and enters the draft, they compare them to Nate Robinson as if Nate is the only little guard that made it in the NBA. You never ever hear anybody being compared to Jose Juan Berea who is smaller and a lot less athletic but his IQ and Skill Level is extremely high. I say that to say this focus on developing IQ and Skill because it's the only thing you can control. Your height and athleticism is not in your control and the point guard position is the one most dependent on IQ.

Books of Influence

Many books raised my antennas the way I'm trying to raise yours. I'll only mention 3. One is "Talent is Overrated" by Geoff Colvin. All 3 books are similar in the message the send. It's all about Mastery and the ways to reach it. In this book, it the main message is that

NOBODY, not one person on this earth, is a master at anything without practicing.

I believe in natural talent but natural talent is just a head start. Without building on it, those who started without it but have a better work ethic will catch and pass those with it that don't build on it. The thing many masters learn that others don't is the concept of "deliberate practice."

It's hard to define but can be explained through examples. The closest definition I can give is, having a specific target or goal before you practice/workout that you haven't hit yet and not leaving until you reach that goal. It may not be fun but if you need a workout to always be fun you'll never be great. Get out of your comfort zone every workout.

Let me give examples...

Below Average Practice

1.   500 Attempts
2.   Count the amount of makes you get in 500 attempts
3.   Beat that score in your next workout

Average Practice

1.   500 Makes

2.   Count the amount of attempts it takes to get 500 makes
3.   Beat that score in your next workout

Deliberate Practice

1.   500 "All-Net" Makes
2.   Count the amount of attempts and/or makes it takes to get   500 "All-Net" makes
3.   Beat that score in your next workout

It's easy to see the separation in the ways of going about mastering your craft. The elite operate under "Deliberate Practice." They challenge themselves more and don't stop until they complete that challenge. Let's look at the above in a different way, time and production. Who will be in the gym for longer and get more reps. 500 makes is good but imagine how many makes you'll get just to get to 500 All-Net? In whatever your normal practice routine is find ways to make it deliberate.

If you're doing combo moves into a jump shot, in what ways can you make it deliberate? After reading the above I know you're thinking make it All-Net makes. Nope. Isolate the move first. Just focus on that alone, sometimes super slow without the ball. Let's say "A" is the combo move and "B" is the jump shot.

One thing I learned is when working most kids out, when you do "A" they can focus on "A" and all its details. Then as soon as you add a "B" to it they seem to forget all the details about "A" because all they're thinking about is "B." That's because "A" is not second nature. We do this a lot as coaches and players, were too quick to add a "B" before "A" is second nature. Isolate both moves and make them second nature before you add them together.

This is necessary because I can't count how many times I tell a kid to do a combo move into a jump shot and they do a step back. Why are you doing stepbacks and you can't do a proper 1 dribble pull up? Or why when I ask you to do a layup you do a eurostep?

Master the basics before you advance. Colleges will not offer kids that can do a euro or a step back if they can't do a basic layup or a proper 1 dribble pull up. Why not? Because in a game there will be more opportunities to do a basic layup and a 1 dribble pull up. Master the basic then move on. 'Deliberate Practice' is not always fun but it's necessary to master any craft.

The 2nd book is "Art of Learning" by Josh Waitzkin. Art of Learning helped me confirm my way of thinking as far as teaching the game. It's about Josh Waitzkin (the subject of the movie "Searching for Bobby Fischer") who was a grandmaster at chess before he was 18. When the celebrity took his love for the game away he quit and started Push-Hands martial arts. He became a world champ at that in just a few years after never doing it before.

After people kept asking him how could he be a world champ in 2 things. He started to think about how he did it. He figured out it was the way he learned. It explains how there is 2 types of learning, entity and incremental. Entity is the type of learning that involves shortcuts and schemes that are not long term paths of success.

Incremental is focusing on the basics and fundamentals and building off that. Learn step 1 make that second nature then move on to step 2 and repeat. This is the long-term way that keeps you successful in whatever avenue you choose to pursue for life. I read the whole book but if I can leave you with something to take from the book to apply to your development, it would be to,
"Learn how you learn best."

Josh talked about another thing that a lot of us not only as coaches and trainers, but also as parents unknowingly do, praise. Every kid needs praise somewhere along the way but the way we do it is wrong a lot of times. While we always praise with good intentions we may be ingraining the mind to be weak when handling adversity.

How do we do this? By praising results rather than the process. When a kid has a good game we may tell them how good they are. We do this instead of telling them they played well because they put the work in and was prepared to play well. By doing this we put in their mind that putting in hours of work is why they're good and why they will be great if they keep working.

Praising results makes the mind weak. If we tell the kid how good they are after a good game they think they were born good as if it is an inherited trait like eye color. So when they face some kind of failure they are confused as to why they're not dominating like they had before. Their confidence takes a hit that they may not be able to rebound from and they don't have the work ethic nor believe in practicing the way they should.

When the kids who are praised for their work ethic faces failure, they think they either didn't prepare the right way or need to practice more. Their confidence isn't shattered it stays the same. Their focus increases. They'll likely have more 'deliberate practice' after failure. Be careful the way you praise because the type of praise you give plays a part in the mindset a kid will obtain.

"Outliers" by Malcolm Gladwell is the 3rd book. The book has a section about the "10,000-hour Theory" that I'm sure you've heard of by now. It states that an anything you do you will not become a master until you have logged 10,000 hours of practice. This provided me with the mindset to not work with anybody that doesn't want to work constantly. Developing greatness is a full-time thing. That's why I study the game psychotically. To the point where I'll see somebody do a move off pure reaction and I'll teach it to my players and make it a habit.

I only know a few dudes' psychotic like me with ball and these dudes are like my brothers from another and they've done some high level developing in this game. Develop continuously and everything will happen the way it is supposed to. Three of the top 5 PG's in the game (Westbrook, Curry, and Lillard) weren't top 100 guys. They were overlooked but they just kept working and things fell in place the way they were supposed to.

All three books influenced my life in a way that makes me really mean it when I say "my life." Now imagine what it can do for you if you apply my explanations to your work ethic. Imagine "Learning how you learn best" then getting in 10,000 hours of "Deliberate Practice" in. I can promise you will develop much faster. But it takes 2 cliché things to do this, dedication and motivation.

The Mental

Growing up I heard the same phrase over and over. The more and more I heard it, the less and less I heard it. Meaning it went in one ear and out the other. The quote I'm talking about is like many other things that our parents, grandparents, aunts, and uncles tell us that we never understand the importance of until we're older. That quote is,

"THE GAME IS 90% MENTAL AND 10% PHYSICAL!"

This paragraph is specifically for the youth really trying to learn the game. That quote is the realest line in this book. Drill this in your head. I'm not some oldhead saying this because it's politically correct. I'm somebody young enough to relate to you enough for you to believe it. Let's go back to the car comparison. Last chapter I talked about your handle being the engine of a car. Well your brain is your engine control unit.

It is basically the cars brain. It controls everything in the car. Without this, the car is useless. Your car may have the best engine, smoothest transition, and the best tires. But if that engine control unit has any malfunctions, your car is just potential instead of production. We all love potential but potential is a fantasy production is reality. Potential can be production if you build your brain to handle all the other parts properly. The rest of this chapter will guide you to building your car.

How to Study Film

Film! The most ignored part of development. I can't understand why, especially in this era. As a Hooper, I always stole. The best players steal from other players. Kobe copied moves from Jordan. Tim Hardaway's "Killer Crossover" is still taught today. Iverson's crossover was copied throughout the league. Dirk's 1 foot fade away is copied by all the elites. So forth and so on.

Everything you need to study the game is on YouTube. You can study any player. You can rewind to see a specific move over and over until you get it. That's a privilege that my generation did not have. But if this is this generation's norm is to have Wi-Fi, iPad, and YouTube how can they appreciate it? Well I'm here to tell you that you should.

Step 1: The way I do it is I setup a gmail (which is needed to sign in to YouTube) specifically for studying the game, and yes, I study the game EVERYDAY!
Step 2: Pick a player to study.
Step 3: Ask these questions. What do they do best? Do they have a "Go-To" move? What are the steps to it?
Step 4: Keep studying that player until you can answer those questions.
Step 5: Add it to your game.
Step 6: Move on to a new player and repeat.

Now be careful who you study! Some players' games are "Athleticism Based" rather than "Skill Based." Skill outlasts athleticism. You'll lose athleticism way before you'll lose skill. For example, there has been a bunch of players, who I won't name, who were top 5 in the league but fell off severely after they lost a step. This is because their games were more athleticism based.

On the other hand, there were players who games were based solely on skill, even when they lost a step they were still productive. So, study the less athletic elite guys. Russell Westbrook is hard to study and steal from. He's so athletic you'll never be able to do what he does. But what you can get from him is mentality.
STUDY THE GAME… EVERYDAY…. IT'S A MAJOR PART OF MASTERING YOUR CRAFT!

Studying You: WHAT DID I? WHY DID I?

When studying yourself, the hardest part is removing your love for yourself. Film is a logical activity not emotional. Many kids that watch game tape on themselves just want to see their highlights. Ask yourself this question, do you only rewind your buckets, assists, and crossovers? Yeah, I figured you did. When watching your personal game, tape look for WHAT AND ASK WHY?

- What turnovers did I have and ask yourself why did I turn the ball over?
- What shots did I miss? And why did I miss them?
- What shots did I pass up on? Why didn't I notice that shot was there for me?
- What passes did I miss? Why did I miss them?
- What rebounds didn't I get? Why didn't I get that them?
- What steals didn't I get? Why didn't I?
- What defensive rotation did I miss? Why did I miss it?

Notice how all I'm talking about is what you didn't do. Understand, watching game tape shouldn't be fun it should be disappointing. You get better by correcting mistakes not celebrating the good things you did do. Get outside of yourself. Watch film as if you're trying to humble your over-confident little brother. So, ask these questions and don't stop replaying clips until you answer those questions.

Studying Us: WHAT DID WE? WHY DID WE?

Next is studying your team film. This is a major part of "Learning your Personnel." This is where you get to examine strengths and weaknesses of the people you go to war. When studying your teammates, you want to figure out everything about them. Tendencies, whether good or bad. Where are they the most and least productive on the floor. Better yet let me rephrase it so you can fully understand the importance of the last statement. Ask yourself "Where can I trust them?"
Remember you're trying to build your car but this is still a team sport. Anything involving 2 or more people with a common goal can only reach that common goal if there is true trust. Also, study your team's' execution of what your coach wants you to do.

- What sets did we execute?
- What sets didn't we execute? Why didn't we execute them?
- What sets did we have trouble guarding? Why did we have trouble guarding them?
- What actions did we have trouble guarding? Why did we have trouble guarding?
- What defensive sets are we weak at? Why are we weak in those sets?

Understanding your team is like playing chess. Understanding the strengths and weaknesses of each piece allows you to better hide your team's weaknesses. You can put your pieces in positions of power. If every piece is in position to perform well, everybody feels part of the win. The trust you build in wins builds accountability in losses. Each piece understands better in a loss what part they played in it. They'll be more likely to admit when they didn't do what they are trusted to do. This in turn makes you stronger in the long term.

Studying Them: WHAT THEY DO? WHY DO THEY DO IT?

I remember when I was coaching at Archbishop Carroll and we played a team out of Chicago with 6 Division 1 players. This team on paper matched up with us equally talent wise. The head coach put me in charge of the scout for this team. Knowing that they matched up well with us I knew that it would pretty much come down to who did the best scout job. I felt a little bit of pressure but I embraced that pressure. I took it as an opportunity to show my basketball knowledge.

To make a long story short we won by 30. I left no details out and this is how I came up with that scouting report. I wrote down these questions before the game so all I had to do was write down the answers when I watched their game. These are the questions I asked that you should ask when scouting an upcoming opponent.

- What is their personnel? Who are their go to guys?
- What are their go to guys' strengths and weaknesses?
- What do they run for their go to guys?
- What is their style of play, in half court or up-tempo?
- Are they good a good rebounding team? How many do they send to the glass?
- Do they run a lot of sets or let their players play freely?
- What sets do they execute the best?

- Do they play 3 out 2 in? DO they play 4 out 1 in? Do they play 5 out?
- How do they defend the pick and roll?
- How good do their bigs slide their feet in the pick & roll?
- Do they play man, zone, or both?
- Do they play full court man, ¾ court man, or ½ court man?
- Do they trap? Where at? Where from?
- Do they zone press?
- What zones do they play?

Knowing your opponents before you step on the court shields you from less surprises. It also helps keep you composed when they make any run during the game. This is key because as a team you can say we knew this was possible this is their identity. Let's do a better job executing the game plan. In a huddle when you didn't scout there would be a lot of panicking and finger pointing which leads to teams folding at the times when you really need to come together.

*How to study templates are in the "Add-On Bundle"

Playing Against Coaches (Game Plan)

Playing D3 wasn't good for my playing career after college but it was the best thing for me as a Coach/Trainer. This was because playing at a level lower than you should be at makes you a bigger threat. In every game I played I was the main guy in every team's scouting report. So, I looked at the game differently.

I wasn't playing against any player on the court I was playing against a coach's game plan. I used to think to myself, "They don't have anybody that can stay in front of me so they're either going to box and 1, throw double teams at me on the baseline, or go zone." This way I was a step ahead. I knew which plays to go to right away depending on what they throw at us. I also know what spots on the floor I'll get my shots at depending on their game plan.

On another note, if you see something, DO NOT be afraid to tell your coach. Plenty of times my coach called something and I said, "Nah coach we going with this, I see something." The mark of true floor general.

One thing every point guard needs to make a habit is getting in the lane. I tell my point guards all the time "Get paint touches. If you see the elbows open attack them." Nothing frustrates an opposing coach more than a guard you can't keep out of the lane.

When coaches put in plays, my mind was so good that I would remember the play immediately. While the other players were just trying to remember the plays, I was already thinking of the counter I can use when the opponent got familiar with the play. When that happened, I would counter and make a play for us when we needed it. Most of the time in the last 5 minutes of a game when we needed a big bucket.

Dealing with Coaches

If you read the "About the Author" section you will notice that I played for many different styles of coaches. I can't name all the types of coaches because everybody is different. However i can hit one point the can help with all coaches. LEARN HOW TO COMPROMISE. You will always run into coaches that will have the "This is all I need you to do" mentality.

The coaches that are not concerned with your long term development. They are only concerned with what they need you to do for them to win. When faced with this you have to learn how to compromise. You have to find that fine line where your style of play and the style they want you to play become bros. I'll give two examples to drive this point home.

In high school my coach made me play off the ball because we needed scoring. If I knew then what I know now I would've asked him could I be the backup point or let me be the point guard in the 4th quarter. Then having the mentality I have I would've made it undeniable that I could be the scorer we needed but at the point guard spot. In college my coach didn't like me shooting 3's. He said I was taking it easy on the defense when I did that. On the other hand I have the mentality where I use threes to open my game. In this example I made him accept it. When I shot it I made sure I made it.

That season I shot 46% from three, the highest on the team. He couldn't really say anything because most of mine were off the dribble. No team helped off of me. He ended up being happy because me using three's opened up my game. This allowed me to make the game easier for everybody because teams had to guard me at half court so I could get in the lane whenever and make plays. Find that line of compromise where you and your coach are happy. Prove you can do the things you want to do so your coach can see it as an asset. If you can't then you have to do it their way until you develop those certain areas to the point where it's undeniable.

Tendencies and Adjustments

To play like a coach on the floor you have to think like a coach on and off the floor. You should learn how to watch and play the game at the same time. This way you'll know the adjustments to make and when to make them. One of my main things was, I completely ran the offense through the first half. I looked to get my teammates in a groove and see who had it going that day so I know who I can really go to in the second half when or if the game gets tight.

Plus, when you get everybody else going it opens the floor for you because instinctively help defenders are scared to help off their man. I wasn't aggressive at all scoring wise in the first half. I only shot open shots and didn't look to create my own shots. I got it within the flow of the offense. Defensively, I just watched what was working for them and watched their players' tendencies.

I did this because in my freshman year I noticed that when I was aggressive in the first half, the second half is when I would see different defenses like a box and 1 or a full court denial. After realizing this tendency, I made the adjustment as stated in the paragraph above. This became my mentality in the game. Basketball was chess and any game plan became fun to beat.

If I'm non-aggressive in the first half I won't be the main factor of your halftime speech. They'll think they have me contained. When I come out in the second half aggressive with adjustments in mind a full or 30 second timeout isn't long enough to make the adjustment needed to stop what we're doing. Learn tendencies and adjust. Rarely will a game plan stay the same throughout the game.

Progressions

Do things in the beginning of the game to open up things for you to finish strong. I used to shoot a long three in the beginning of the game to open up my drive game. If they see me shoot it from deep they would think, "He must be able to shoot if he shooting from that far." From there I can do whatever I want because you have to come out and play me past the 3. The floor is now open for me to maneuver through all 4 levels freely.

Another progression is from the 3 to the drive or the drive to the 3. If you hit a 3 early they have to close out hard, on a closeout you now have the 1 dribble pull up. After that you have the drive or dump off pass because the bigs will now closeout hard on the 1 dribble pull up. If you drove, then next you'll have the floater because the big will be cautious about you getting all the way to the rim or dumping it off to his man. But if you dumped it off you'll still have the floater. Once you start to realize how the things you've done in the past will affect how the defense will react to you on the next play, you're a step ahead and in control.

As a guard, I was never worried about who was in front of me. I was so confident that I never even thought about that. My thoughts were,

"When I get by him, where would the help come from?"

If I know where they are beforehand I'll have an idea of what may happen when I get there, advantage US! I don't come off of a ball screen or attack a defender one on one until I know where EVERYBODY on the court is. Think about how a road trip would be without a GPS. You wouldn't know the right route to go avoid standstill traffic. Go when you know roads are clear because everybody loves a smooth trip.

Just make sure that you start thinking about how the things you just did will open things up for you in the next few possessions. I always tell kids that I work out,

"Do not do anything if you don't have a counter off of it."

Short Term Memory

In all the games I've played in, coached, and watched I've never seen anybody play a perfect game. So it confuses me to see somebody still mad at the last play that didn't go so well. Whether it's a turnover, missed shot, dropped pass, or bad call, MOVE ON! You have to have a "Next Play Mentality." I hate to see somebody turn the ball over get mad and foul whoever stole the ball from them not knowing that theyre are in the bonus.

Because you can't get out of your emotions quickly you gave up a the potential for a 4 or 5 point swing. It's a 4 or 5 point swing because you turned it over which could've resulted in a 2 or 3 pointer. Then you fouled which gives them a chance at 2 points. If you had a "Next Play Mentality" you would've got over it immediately and hustled back and played defense.

When I train kids and they get mad because they're not picking up something quickly, I stop and have a conversation with them. I tell them all the same thing,

"Nothing that I am doing with you is something that you mastered and if you did we wouldn't be doing it anymore. So why are you mad that you can't do something perfectly every rep that you didn't master yet? Get out of your feelings and be honest with yourself. The reason you're not doing any reps perfectly is because your mind is on your last rep in a bad way. The last rep is only used for information. It should let you know in your mind what you did wrong so you know what to correct the next rep or tell you to do it the way I did it the last rep. DON'T GET MAD! GET MORE FOCUSED!"

Usually after this 1 minute conversation the quality of the workout doubles. Not to keep using the same word but it goes from an average workout to "deliberate practice." The best part about the conversation is we never have to have the conversation again. When they lose focus, I start to say one line from the convo that gets them right back on track,

"DON'T GET MAD! GET MORE FOCUSED!"

This is having that "Next Play Mentality" that the greatest have. Reggie Miller who is one of the top 3 shooters of all time, no debate, is quoted saying when asked about a shooting slump, "Keep shooting, again and again and again, as long as it takes."

Kobe Bryant, top 5 player of all time and known for his mentality and confidence, has stated, "I would go 0-30 before I would go 0-9. 0-9 means you beat yourself, you psyched yourself out of the game."

Michael Jordan, the G.O.A.T, stated, I've missed more than 9000 shots in my career. I've lost almost 300 games.

26 times, I've been trusted to take the game winning shot and missed. I've failed over and over and over again in my life. And that is why I succeed."

You get the point. Last season, game, and play is just something to learn from not to be stuck on. Letting go allows for growth, but learning from and letting go speeds up growth. From the quotes above you see that the greats of the game have a next play mentality in whatever they do. They let nothing affect their confidence. So what's your reason for doing so? Like I said,

"DON'T GET MAD! GET MORE FOCUSED!"

The Physical

Skill development Is the most important thing in any sport. Without skill development, nothing you read before or after this section means anything. Like I said in the beginning of the chapter "Outliers" by Malcolm Gladwell is one of my favorite books. I truly believe in the "10,000 Hour Theory." How can you not?

If you don't believe in it just think about this, if you put in 10,000 hours of practice imagine how good you will be even if they're not a master. In the NBA, the guys who are All-Stars year after year are in the gym day after day working on something new. They understand that there are no shortcuts to being a master. You got to lace up, get in the gym, and put in work.

There are 2 key components to developing skill, practice and game experience. The yin and yang. The perfect marriage. They keep each other informed on what each other should be doing more or less of. The ultimate measuring stick. If you spend all your time practicing when you get in a game setting you will not dominate the way you expect too. Your timing will be off and there's actually people trying to stop you, not some imaginary defender you score on every rep.

Practice is key for preparing you for most game situations but it never prepares you for all. The feel for the game will take time to acquire. What I will say is, when the feel for the game meets the skill development you will be a problem. On the other hand, if all you do is play games and barely get in skill development no matter how naturally talented to you are eventually everybody will catch you. Your development will be very slow with no peaks. The game will always tell you if you're not in the gym enough or if you need to up the level you're playing in you just need to keep your eyes and ears open when the game is trying to speak to you.

When it comes to skill development and game experience, they should be managed properly. Skill development should be an everyday thing. The games should be 2-3 days a week but always challenging. You should never be playing at a level where you can dominate. The more challenging the game the more the hunger stays alive when developing skill. If you're playing at a level where you can't dominate, there's no room to get cocky.

Your level of focus will always be there. This is deliberate practice within a game setting. If you're a player reading this take this advice immediately, if you're bored up your level. If you're a parent, coach, or trainer working with a kid, make sure the player you're working with is not bored. Boredom breeds laziness in basketball. You start to feel like you don't need to keep putting in the same work.

If you're dominating your age group, you need to move up in age group immediately. For example, in AAU most of the guys in the top 100 in their class play up a year in age. Either the kid wants to or the AAU Program Directors do this for the reason I just stated. Many players play their age and by the time they get to 17 and Under their stock dropped and they're wondering why. Well it dropped because they didn't develop much because there has been no challenge which keeps the hunger alive.

Let's put things in perspective of skill development and Game experience time put in relative to the "10,000 Hour Theory of Mastery"

----

2 hours a day * 6 days a week = 12 hours a week
12 hours a week * 52 weeks in a year = 624 hours in year
10,000 hours / 624 hours a year = 16.02 years to be a Master

3 hours a day * 6 days a week = 18 hours a week

18 hours a week * 52 weeks in a year = 936 hours in year
10,000 hours / 936 hours a year = 10.68 years to be a Master

4 hours a day * 6 days a week = 24 hours a week
24 hours a week * 52 weeks in a year = 1,248 hours in year
10,000 hours / 1,248 hours a year = 8.01 years to be a Master

----

1 extra hour a day changes the speed of development by years. If that's not enough to make you want to step up your work ethic, then you just don't have the drive to be great. If that's the case stop reading if you haven't already.

POSITIONLESS: Train as a Point Guard!

When it comes to skill development there is some things that every player, coach, or trainer needs to know. Every kid should be trained as a point guard! There are 2 reasons for this, size and positionless. By size I mean, you never know how tall you are going to be. You can get your kids growth plates checked. But if you ever heard of Johnny Flynn the former point guard for Syracuse and the Timberwolves, you know he's 6'0 but was supposed to be 6'5. He broke a limb when he was younger that caused him not to fully grow to 6'5. However he was a point guard all his life so he still made the league. TRAIN AS A POINT GUARD!

If you ever heard of Anthony Davis for the Pelicans you know he was a barely recruited 6'2 guard as a sophomore in high school. He grew to 6'11 and was the #1 player in the country easily. Why? Because he had guard skills and mobility. A point guard can transition into a center easier than a center can transition into point guard. Once again, TRAIN AS A POINT GUARD!

By now we all heard the term "Positionless" unless you been under a rock the past 5 years. This is where the game is going like it or not. The game is getting faster and faster. In the mid 2000's Mike D'Antoni introduced the NBA to his "7 seconds or less" system it was the most exciting offense in the league. It involved getting the ball up the floor in 7 seconds and running a lot of pick & roll. The Suns won 62 games one year and D'Antoni won coach of the year. However nobody believed that system could win a championship. Well they were right, and wrong!

They were right at the time but they were wrong because the Warriors run a similar system and won a championship. This is where the game is going now, faster and faster. Train as a point guard because nobody is throwing the ball in the low post all game and giving somebody 7 seconds to get a shot up. Look at the Sixers. They drafted Jahlil Okafor and Joel Embiid. Okafor is a monster in the low post and so is Embiid. However, the low post is where Okafor game stays, Embiid can shoot the 3 and take other bigs off the dribble and make a play. Because of how the game is going Okafor is on the trading block.

Back to the Warriors, if you've been watching them you'll notice that their point guard is Draymond Green. Why? Because he is their best rebounder and one of their best passers. How dangerous is a team whose best rebounder can get it off the glass and push the ball and make the right play. Also that means the 2 best shooters can get up the floor and get shots up quickly. How do you guard a team who is "Positionless?"

Look at Giannis Antetokounmpo he's the same thing but even worse, he's 6'11. Honestly besides Westbrook, he's my 2nd favorite player. I believe he can be the best player in the world. I said it last year and everybody looked at me crazy and said "He ok." Or, "He got potential but I don't know about all that." Well look now, he's an All Star this year.

Lebron is getting old and he can play and guard the 1-5. How can you tell me he can't be the best in the game at some point in his career. The game is becoming "Positionless" and he's a 22 year old All Star without a position. I don't want to get too deep into it but you better TRAIN AS A POINT GUARD! Soon you're going to have to be able to do everything to be able to get in the league.

Let's change pace a bit. Basketball is all about reading and reacting. Counters is another word for it. Like I said in the 'Progressions' section, do not do anything offensively if you don't have a counter off of it. Your game will never be all it can be until your game becomes all reaction. You're supposed to think during the game, but not when it comes to moves. The game has to be reaction. Train to make things second nature so you don't have to think, YOU

JUST DO. Build the right habits. Like I said before, don't move on to "A" until "B" is second nature. Trying to learn everything at once will keep you stagnated in your development.

If you've seen pros like Kobe, KD, or Demar Derozan workout you'll notice they maybe just working on one move for a whole workout. Why? Because whatever they are working is a move they have not mastered that they feel they need to. Also, all the other moves that lead up to that progression have been mastered. They understand how deliberate practice on one move is better for long term development.

To be the best player you can be, steal from the best. To be a great finisher, study the best finishers. To be a great shooter, study the best shooters. To be a great shot creator, study the best shot creators. To be a great ball handler, study the best ball handlers. If you don't get the message by now, it's take one thing and focus on making that a habit then move on.

One thing you need to know is, mistakes are actually your best friend. Of course you want to get it right every time. But the truth is, you never will get everything 100% right 100% of the time. Mistakes allow your brain struggle and as the slogan goes, no struggle, no progress. If you get something wrong and your response is to figure it out, then guess what, you're going to figure it out.

Be honest with yourself. You're going to make mistakes! You'll make them in the game, at practice, and in life. So change your relationship in response to mistakes. A mistake should be your friend that's telling you, "You almost got it, keep working. Not the friend that makes you mad telling you, "Just quit, your never going to get it."

Reps

When training, I religiously yell out the details of what we're doing. Even to the point where I'm tired of hearing myself. However it's necessary to be a good trainer. One reason is, it becomes subconscious in the player's mind. They start to say it to themselves as they are going through a rep. In one rep I'll tell them the details they got right and wrong. They start to feel when they got a detail right. This also means that they start to feel when they got it wrong. That's the second and most important reason I do it. It will get to a point where they go through a rep and and stop mid-rep and immediately knowing why they stopped I'll ask,

"Why you stop?"
"I got the second part wrong."

At this point, my job as a teacher is over because they can correctly correct themselves. I now change my role from teacher to encourager. This now becomes something that they can do by themselves. Once you get to this point on any specific skill you can focus on getting enough reps to make it a habit. That's the process,

1. Learn the correct details for a specific skill
2. Get the feel for right and wrong
3. Then get enough reps to make it a habit

There's no shortcut. That's it, believe it or not. The only time to combine things is if "A" and "B" is second nature,

"C" is almost a habit, and the whole combination is game specific. That's another aspect of it that you want to put into your training, game specific. I believe in this but to a certain degree. That should happen in the middle school stages. When younger, you should be doing just "A" to make the basic fundamentals second nature.

For example, before you work on a killer crossover make sure the crossover and the through the legs dribble is smooth separately. Then as you get better you can do a killer crossover into a euro step and finish with the outside hand. You see what I mean? That play is beautiful when it can be completed perfectly. It'll look effortless and give people the feel that you're just naturally talented.

That's what happens when you make things second nature it looks effortless or better yet thoughtless. There was, in fact, no thought involved because it was second nature, it was a reaction. Remember, train to make things second nature so you'll always have the correct reaction. Its funny how we're talking about training which is a physical thing, but the discussion is mostly mental. The oldheads were not lying, 90% mental 10% physical.

Building the Body NOT Body Building

Getting stronger is a problem for a lot of players. Lack of strength takes away many things in your game. First of all, basketball is a contact sport. You're going to get hit. If you're scared to get hit, QUIT NOW! Layups are a big part of the game. On your way to the rim you'll get contact and once you get to rim you'll get more contact.

Rebounds are a big part of the game. When going for a rebound nobody cares about anything but getting the ball therefore elbows are flying. You see what I'm getting at? You can't dodge it so you better get prepared for all the physicality basketball will bring. I'm not going to act like I went to school for Kinesiology even though I plan on it, but I can share with you what worked for me and players that I trained over the years.

Before Puberty

In my opinion, you shouldn't be doing any workouts involving weights until around 11th grade. My reason for this is, I figured out through research that proper body mechanics is overlooked. Too many times have I worked high school or older and they played very upright. I would keep saying "You gotta get lower." Almost every time they would reply, "I'm trying but I can't."

After being tired of hearing this and not knowing how to fix it I did research and found out it's because their core, hips, glutes, and hamstrings weren't activated. Focus on this because you don't need weights to work on the most important thing you need in basketball. You need to look on YouTube and research "hip activation", "glute activation", "hamstring activation", and "core activation."

Focus early on building proper body mechanics. The lower you can play the harder you are to guard. To give you an idea of something I teach that makes it simple for even a 6-year-old. When I want to teach a player that can play lower but their playing upright. I simply say if you want to get by anybody you have to get your shoulder by me. Sometimes they say, "I never thought of it like that."

Then I explain that to do that easier than they do it they have to lower their shoulder when they're trying to go by somebody. If you play upright, even when you get by a defender if they give you a little bit of contact they can knock you off balance enough to get back in front of you. But if you play with a low center of gravity, when you get by them and they give you a bump it won't phase you at all.

Let's go back to the car analogy. Your center of gravity is your wheelbase which means how far apart your wheels are from each other. If your car is upright with a narrow wheel base like a 15-passenger van, it's easier to flip over in an accident. However, if your car is low to the ground with a wider wheelbase you have a way better chance at not being flipped over. Besides offensively the lower your center of gravity and quicker you are laterally allowing you to lock down whoever you're guarding. We all know defense wins most championships.

Another benefit of activating the hamstrings, core, hips, and glutes is injury prevention. The most you will need to activate your hips, core, hamstrings and glutes is a resistance band. Once you find a routine you should be doing these activations 3 to 4 times a week. GET STARTED!

Upper Body Pre-Puberty

When it comes to the upper body the most important groups in my opinion are the shoulder and triceps. The shoulders allow you to give out contact on your way to the basket and give out strong enough contact on a layup to neutralize a big man's length. Notice how many times the best finishers like Westbrook, Kyrie, Lebron, and Harden use their shoulders to get to the basket and finish. The triceps are important for ease of shooting, the stronger your triceps the more you can extend your range while not having to change your shot. Don't get me wrong the chest, back and biceps are important but you use the shoulders and triceps more.

I recommend different variations of:
- Push-ups
- Pull-ups
- Dips

Also, look up shoulder push-ups. Once this gets easy start using a resistance bands for more of challenge. Develop a routine of these different variations 4 to 5 times a week and always switch it up after 3 weeks because you plateau when your muscles get used to a routine. Around 3 weeks is always a good time to trick your muscles.

Lower Body Pre-Puberty

Plyometrics is a major thing in basketball. Always was and always will be. Every kid wants to jump like Russell Westbrook. While most think it's impossible it basically is because they start too late. You want to develop quick twitch early. Some of the exercises I know to be effective are:
- Lunges
- Lateral Lunges
- Lateral Hops
- Squats

- Jump Squats
- Box Jumps
- Agility Ladder Drills

Weightlifting: Post Puberty

Once you hit 11th grade this is when I suggest you start hitting the weights hard. For one like most you've probably are far enough past your first stage of puberty. Second, your last year of AAU is coming up and you want to be physically ready for that. I've coached 15 and under to 17 and under and speed and strength take a major step every year you move up.

If you can get a personal trainer do so. If not do your research on how to properly lift so you don't injure yourself. Remember, basketball is not a stiff sport so bodybuilding is not the goal. Getting stronger while keeping your same speed and agility is key.

If you know about the combines, then you know the NFL combine tests strength by having the players lift 225lb but the NBA only does 185lb. You want to get as strong as you can but you don't want to get too big. Lean muscle is what you're looking for. By this time, you should be a great athlete due to focusing on body mechanics first. You should be lifting 3-4 times a week and switch up your routine every 3 weeks.

Conditioning

Conditioning is something that you can do like a pro when you're in elementary. I'm a different type of guy I always like to think outside of the box. While running miles and sprints are essential, there are other things that are tougher for you that also build muscular endurance. Running hills, running steps, and cycling whether it's in a class or on the street. When you need to make it tougher you can add things like a weight vest, parachute, and/or altitude mask.

One thing a lot of coaches make their team do is run cross country. If your coach doesn't make you do it then you should make yourself do it. Keep this in mind, nobody likes to come out of the game, if you're in great shape, your coach may not take you out. As a coach, I have taken out players many times not because they were tired but because I needed them in them to finish the game out strong. This is how you can be the player coach doesn't need to take out. Develop a routine to do at least 4 to 5 times a week.

To make it fun to do conditioning, get a heavy ball, put your headphones on, put your music on shuffle, and dribble while running around your neighborhood. At some point during your run you'll zone out. You'll forget you're actually running and be in deliberate practice mode. You'll be treating everything you're running by as a defender and having fun with it. I really recommend this for the younger kids because it kind of tricks them into conditioning. They'll be thinking about doing moves and not running. Keep it creative!

Taking Care of the Body: Recovery

The body throughout this journey will go through stages that make you say "I need a week off." No, you need to take care of your body correctly after a workout. Taking the time to do so after a workout can mean being able to workout on Tuesday after a hard workout on Monday rather than waiting until Thursday because you're too sore. That's 2-3 days of work you missed. Under the 10,000-hour theory that's about 6 hours you missed. You're 6 hours behind being a master and with the way athletes are being bred today you shouldn't be a minute late.

Some of the basics of recovery are drinking water, whey protein, proper sleep, and chocolate milk. Chocolate milk contains the type of protein that helps muscles recover. The basic ways to recover is ice baths, epsom salt baths, and foam rolling. Some advanced ways to recover are cryotherapy, sauna room, and ice baths. You don't have to be a pro to train like a pro and if you train like a pro early enough you'll be a pro. But with training like a pro you have to take care of your body to be able to train like a pro.

Stretching

Stretching is key for flexibility and preventing injuries. Many times, it's not done right though. You must know the types of stretching and how to properly do them. There are two types, static and dynamic. Static is when you get in a certain position and hold for 10-20 seconds. Dynamic is when you are doing movements to stretch the muscles and getting the blood flowing while you're doing so. Both are very necessary but should be done at different times.

Static is known to lengthen muscle tissue but also decreases strength and power so it shouldn't be done before a game, practice or workout. It should be done after a game, practice, or at home before sleep. Develop a routine that is done 3 days a week for 20 to 30 minutes. Before each stretch jog or do jumping jacks if you are home to get the blood flowing. Taking yoga classes is also a very good idea. I have many of my guys' I train take yoga classes and many NBA guys do also.

Dynamic on the other hand decreases stiffness, maximizes performance, and lessens the possibility of injury. This is to be done before every game, practice, or workout. You'll see this at any College or NBA game you attend.

<u>Nutrition</u>

Metabolism has a way of working against us. When were young its super-fast so it burns off any thing we eat very fast. No matter how bad the food we eat is for us we never realize it until it's too late. Once we hit adulthood and the metabolism slows down the same foods we've been eating that was not hurting us has a different effect, or so we thought.

The foods were always bad for us but our basal metabolic rate (the scientific term for it) tricked us. Once it slows down you have less energy in your day to day, add on weight easier, and then you want to change your diet. Understanding metabolism and what stimulates it then you'll take it more serious earlier. It takes a long time to stop habits and a bad diet is one of the hardest habits to break.

Let's go back to the car analogy again. The food and drinks you consume is the gas your car needs to stay running at maximum possible performance. Let's be clear premium gas only benefits luxury and sports cars, but isn't that what we're aiming to be? So why not fuel the way you're supposed to as early as you can. Let's begin with the drinks. Water, the thing that takes up more than half of the body's content is severely ignored.

I'm not going to say drink a gallon a day but you should be close to it as an athlete. I went to a tournament to watch one of the guys I coached who plays for IMG Academy. IMG is top of the line when it comes to the study of sports performance and when you look at their bench you'll see that every player has a gallon of water to themselves. Water flushes toxins, burns calories, boosts metabolism, decreases headaches, and prevents us from overeating. It's essential to not only athletics but life.

We as athletes fell into the trap of sports drinks. The sports drinks are good during a game, practice, or workout not before or after. You need to replace what you lost and an intense workout potassium which is in Gatorade prevents muscle cramping. When building, muscle take a protein shake within 30 minutes' post workout. When it comes to liquids drink all the above at the recommended time. Keep sodas and juices to a minimum. In no way are they good for you but you do need sugar from time to time but don't make them a daily habit.

When it comes to food the athlete Protein and Carbohydrates are key. Protein should be in every meal. Chicken, Non-farmed fish, grass fed beef, eggs, turkey, yogurt, and peanut butter. Make sure your food is grilled or baked. Fried greasy foods are very bad for the diet. I love fried chicken. Grew up on it, so I know how hard it is to turn down 4 wings with hot sauce, but stick to the script at hand.

With carbohydrates focus on complex carbs like fruits, vegetables, oatmeal, and sweet potatoes pre-workout. Simple carbs are only for post workout and should be kept to a minimum. Simple carbs consist of things foods containing heavy sugars and white bread.

Supplements

Supplements should be kept to a minimum because truthfully if you eat and drink right your body will get everything it needs. Whey protein after a muscle building workout and multivitamins every day are the only things you need. Many people look to get a bunch of different supplements to get what the body needs while keeping their same bad diet, what's the point? Supplements have great results when your diet is on point. So, don't try to shortcut the process stick to the long-term path to greatness.

About The Author
What Makes Me Credible

DISCLAIMER: Names of people and places are excluded in the next few sections. This story is to be told to prove why I'm credible for you to take my advice in this particular subject. The intent of this is not to stir up controversy. I have respect for everybody I will speak about in this short story. I appreciate the page they wrote in the book of my life. So names and names of schools are only included if it is absolutely necessary to show my credibility.

This section is just to explain where my love for the position started and what makes me credible to even write this book. To start I've been coaching for about 6 years now, BUT, in this 6 years I have seen basketball in abundance and at a high level. Also, I have been training for about 8 years. Coaching wise I have been with Under Armour Sponsored We-R1 for 4 years now. The best and most consistent program the last 5 years.

I've won the 17u championship 2 years in a row as an assistant. No program on any circuit has ever done so. I've seen and worked with dozens of Division 1 products. I also coached at Archbishop Carroll High School outside of Philly which at one time was top 25 and totaled 7 division 1 players. I have worked with 2 of the top 3 point guards, class of 2017 McDonald's All-Americans. To sum it up I've seen what they call "It", worked with "It", and know what "It" looks like when I see "it".

Elementary: Why I Love The Position

My first love was football. I Thought I was going to the NFL lol. Barry Sanders (The greatest running back of all time, NO DEBATE!) was my favorite player and that's who I wanted to be. Around the same time I realized I wasn't fast enough to be Barry Sanders I started liking basketball more and more. I remember sitting in the kitchen which seemed like every weekend watching the 95 Orlando Magic with Penny and Shaq.

Penny is the reason I played and fell in love with the game. I wasn't fast enough to be Barry Sanders but I felt like I could be Penny. Even to this day my older cousin who was already more into basketball still brings up when I told him a about Penny before he knew about him. It's no coincidence that became his favorite player also. He was that good, something the league had never seen at the time.

After I realized basketball was my thing, I started to work on it more and more. Now unlike the kids I train, we didn't have oldheads that really schooled us and showed us how to work on our game. So I didn't exactly work on my game in the stereotypical way. I would just wake up go to the court and practice moves. On the way to the court I used to dribble the ball and try not to step on the cracks in the sidewalk and use everything on the way to the courts as a defender. What I realize now is this is what made me able to teach so easily today.

That's what gave me the footwork I have still today. Add in me thinking I was Barry Sanders in football. When I first started to hoop I was trying to juke people while dribbling lol. So all elementary all I did was practice moves like the "Killer Crossover, AI crossover, and the "Running Man" a playground move that was known in Philly back in the day. Other than that, I would play all day, until my summer league game in my neighborhood.

The summer league in my hood kept my love for the game going. It was like a baby Rucker. I'm from Darby Township, Pennsylvania on the border of Philly but on the mail it says Sharon Hill, PA because we don't have our own post office. Philly is 5 minutes away and Chester, a small city that's in the running for the state championships every year and produced plenty of ball players that made it to the league and overseas, is 20 minutes away. They also have a bunch of dudes that should've made it but didn't and those dudes played in the league around my way.

This league had everything the game is missing today. Dudes snapping on the ref. People in the crowd talking "ish." No room on the court because everybody watching is basically standing on the court. People in the crowd talking ish with the players and betting on the games. Dudes saying, "I'm going to the trunk," when they got into it with somebody. Basically, everything you need for a good summer league minus the shootings. All the things this generation misses, Basketball only built for the toughest. Where you went to war on the court because you can't have the hood saying you got your ass bust.

After all that, around 11 at night I would go to the courts around my way and play against all the hustlers. The hustlers were nice just never made it for the usual reason, grades, no support system, and/or got in trouble. Just about all of them played in the summer league. I was young but I could play with them because I had a crazy handle so even though they were older they couldn't steal the ball from me, I had dimes, and most importantly I wasn't soft or intimidated. So, that was my game in my elementary days, Flashy, all crossovers and dimes.

Middle School

Once middle school hit I had complete confidence. By this time, I heard I was nice around my way plenty of times. That's what all kids want to hear around that age. I had a natural jump shot without working on it so I had that to open my game up. But the biggest thing I could remember in my development was the "And 1 Mixtapes." Being a coach I can understand another coach reading this and thinking, "What? That's the worst thing for a kids' development." Well, once again the closed minded basketball purist are wrong!

Those mixtapes were the best thing for the imagination. They let you know you weren't that good but didn't kill your confidence. It made you want to be good enough to do what you want, when you want, however you want. The reason people thought they were so bad for the game is, you started to see a lot of people want to cross somebody over and that was it. That was their equivalent to scoring. I was always the kid saying, "All he got is a handle."

I would say this because some people were getting labeled as good just because they had a handle. I played against plenty of dudes who had a crazy handle and ran down on them. Its different when somebody got a crazy handle but uses it to produce. After I crossed somebody over I wanted to finish the play. Those tapes just made me want to get my handle up and figure out how to add more flash without being over the top.

In 8th grade I moved a town over so I went to a new school. That summer i used to go to the courts out there to get my name up. I did that easily and let everybody know where I was from in the process. The school I played for in

7th grade beat the school I went to in 8th by 20. But I got cut from the team. Not because I wasn't good though.

At tryouts I was forced into a role that wasn't me and it made me look bad. What you see at tryouts anywhere in the world is those guys that are non-aggressive and scared to make mistakes so they are passive. Well I had a team full of them and they did it when we went against the starting five from the year before.

Natural basketball instinct kicked in and I just went into scoring mode. Plus I wanted to let them know that none of them was better than me. This led to the coach calling me a "ball hog" and cutting me. That's funny because my whole life I was the best and most willing passer I knew lol. When the list came out everybody was shocked. Nobody clowned me or anything because they knew what it was. It was easily one of the best things that happened to me development wise though.

Since I got cut I played in the Pal league with all the high school kids. Being 5'0 and a 135lbs I was once again in a position where I had to be crafty. Size and athleticism wasn't in my favor playing against the older dudes. I started to use my jumper more to set up my game. I became even more deceptive. I look back now and know that I went into 9th grade better than I would have if I actually made the team.

High School

My high school experience was a roller coaster. To start I was still 5'0 in 9th grade. I made the freshman team, started a lot of games, and didn't start in some. The coach

thought I was too small and too flashy at times. I
remember one day at practice I was on the break in a one
on one situation with somebody way bigger than me.
When I got to the rim, I jumped up and spun around and
pitched it back to a teammate for an easy layup.

**My coach said, "Why would you put yourself in a
position like that?"**
Me, "What position?"
**Coach, "You jumped up and spun around because you
didn't have a shot, luckily he was there."**
**Me, "Nah I did that to get him in the air because I
knew I had a trailer."**
Coach, "What if he wasn't there?"
Me, "I knew he was there."
**Coach, "What if somebody was hustling back into the
play?"**
Me, "I wouldn't have done it."

My coach knew I had talent but he was a textbook coach
so he didn't understand that some people are just that crafty
or they do certain things in a flashy way because that was
the only way to get it don't in that split second. By this
stage I wasn't thinking about doing moves before I did
them (what you see in a lot in High School and AAU
games). I started letting the game come to me. Playing of
off pure reaction. I tell players all the time just keep it
simple and the highlights will happen off of natural
reaction.

My coaches coaching style stunts growth and creativity.
It's cool because he was the last coach I had like that for a
long time after. What really had me mad more than
anything about 9th grade was my growth spurt. The season

was over at the end of February. By the middle of April I went from 5'0 to 5'10. That summer was fun though because growing took my game to another level.

In 10th grade, I made JV because I outplayed the varsity point guard at tryouts. I don't sound excited because I really wasn't. I didn't think he was as good as everybody else did. In my first game, I remember my mom's husband seeing me play for the first time and saying,

"You had a real good game, 14 assists, but you don't shoot enough."

I still didn't care about scoring much plus we won by 20. After the Christmas break, I transferred to American Christian.

The school I was at seemed like they were into a social promotion type of thing when it came to starters and minutes. I wasn't with it. At American Christian I played JV one game so they can feel me out. I had 26 at halftime and was immediately on varsity that same day. The rest of the season went okay. I was held back because they had starters and people they recruited and I came in the middle of the season so I understood.

The best part about 10th grade was that summer going to 11th. Played in the Sonny Hill League. This league can never be duplicated. Every game was a battle. Being from "The County" the city dudes always thought we was sweet (lol). They learned quick that's not always true. Me and my man was right at these dudes every game. Not saying we were dominating because EVERY game was a battle. But we definitely held our own.

This was my introduction to the real basketball underworld. I say that because I finally got to play against dudes that had a name. What I found was a lot of them was gassed and had politics in their favor. Not too say they was terrible because before anything they played hard. But if they played for the right team, worked out with the right guy, and knew the right people they got a name.

I got over on a lot of them dudes but I didn't know the right people and I didn't play AAU. Where I'm from nobody had connections in the city for us to play AAU. I didn't know about any tryouts or anything. There wasn't social media that allows you to know when teams had tryouts, unlucky me.

Going into 11th grade I was about 6'0. I decided I was going to score more. I wanted to have a more well-rounded game. Because you only get noticed when you put points on the board unless you're on a loaded team that play in big tournaments. That year we had a new coach and I liked him from the start. He liked players that can boogie. He would literally call an Iso for you to go at somebody. This is the start of me turning into a killer.

I had the backing by my coach to play my game. Nothing like knowing your coach believes in your game. So, that year I had a couple triple doubles and had real good games against loaded prep school teams. Most of the time we got smacked. But knowing you can go toe to toe with teams with division 1 players gives you confidence.

The most significant thing about 11th grade and maybe my basketball life, happened one day after practice. We had a 7th grader that was our 6th man, yes, a 7th grader was our

6th man. I noticed he never went home after practice so I asked him one day where does he go after practice. He told me he goes to work out with his older brother. I already knew of his brother, he played in the summer league around my way and was always one of the best players.

He asked me if I wanted to go and said yeah but I can't go today my mom is already on her way (back then we didn't have cell phones). So, I told him I would go the next day. After practice the next day I went with him to go workout. We walk in the gym, stretch, and then this 7th Grader says,

"Let's start with 300 3's."
Me in shock, "300 shots?"
Him, "Naw makes"

At this point I said to myself, "He going to the league." I knew this because I never did that before and I was in 11th grade. I didn't know how to workout. Never had an idea of how to go about it. Yet this 7th grader starts his workout with 300 makes and he's 4 years younger than me and has been doing this years before I even did it once. I was correct when I said he was going to the league, that 7th grader was Tyreke Evans.

That summer I realized I was even more behind when my high school coach took us to a Prep School camp. It was players from all the top prep schools like Laurinburg Institute, Mt. Zion, and Lutherans Prep. They also had a lot of dudes from the Top 100 Nike Camp in Canada. The first day I got cool with a funny dude from South Jersey and the only 9th grader at the camp who was from D.C. The kid from D.C. (Who I called "Youngbul" which is a Philly term when you talk about somebody younger than you) was real quiet.

I didn't know if he was good at all. But he was 6'6 and the only 9th grader there so I figured he had to be. I thought he was a big man until I seen him grab a rebound push the break, weave through traffic, take off from the foul line, and finish with a smooth finger roll . I thought I seen it all after seeing how good Reke was and the work he put in but I seen "It" again.

This kid was super long, quick, had a handle, and smooth fluid jumper. Once again, I said to myself, "He going to the league." Two years later a high school game was on ESPN. Oak Hill was playing somebody and when they were talking about all the ranked kids playing in that game they started talking about the #2 player in the country, I yelled out, "That's my youngbul." Yeah, youngbul was Kevin Durant.

At the end of that summer, two of my friends had been working out at the school I left in 10th grade. They were working out with the new Head Coach. The new coach was a legend at the school. He was the all-time leading scorer and got the school the deepest they ever been in the state tournament. But I didn't know him so I wasn't excited. They wanted me to come to workout the next day. By this time, I told you I seen "It" and "It" worked out every day so of course I wanted to workout.

We get there 7 o'clock in the morning and the coach made us run a mile. This was a new progression to my development because I never done that before. Then we go in the gym and run through some drills. I was murdering the drills he had us doing. Anything he was throwing at us I was doing easily. I knew I was because by the time we got to the 3rd drill he stops the drill and says,

"Yo, you live in Darby?"
Me, "Yeah."
Coach,"You gotta come back and be my point guard!"

I thought about it and decided to come back and play with my guys. Mainly because I was going to be the full time point and the league we played was like the old school Big East of Pennsylvania. We had a transfer coming back who went to the school in 9th grade just like me who the coach thought was going to be the extra scorer we needed. Well at least that's what we all thought. He didn't score the way we thought so coach moved me to the 2. His words were,

"You get anywhere you want on the floor but you pass it, usually to people who not gon finish the play."

He was right but he also gassed me (lol). As a kid who was not ranked, had no offers, and no older basketball guidance who was I not to listen to the best player ever at the school? It was just one of those situations where it was what the team needed but not good for my long-term development, so I thought.

What ended up happening was two things… for one, I really turned into a killer. That was the biggest year of development I had. Coach took my game to another level. He told me to let it go if they gave me any space. Well that led to me being arguably the best shooter in the county. I had a game where I hit 8 threes' in a half and plenty more with 5 plus three's.

The second part of it was continuous workouts and competition. We worked out with 2 other high schools 2 to 3 days a week. When you work every day, you start to feel funny when you miss a day. We didn't miss many days. We either worked out on our own or the other two schools, Imhotep Charter and Harriton High School. The coaches of those schools have state chips and deep playoff runs year after year. It's safe to say ball became life that year and it rounded out my game.

That spring I played AAU for the first time because unsigned players can play in the first live period. My team went to Charlie Weber Invitational in D.C. This was one of the biggest tournaments in the early 2000's. From that tournament, I had interest from 3 Low Division 1's. They all told my coach the same thing, "We're interested but we're out of scholarships so he can walk on and redshirt." To me that was a scholarship (lol).

College

Out of those 3 schools I had to pick one and I picked the cheapest school. Pretty much because I didn't know anything about financial aid. I should've picked the school that was interested the most. Ironically the school that cost the most was the most interested and had better basketball and academics. Well that didn't pan out. I had a meeting with the head coach and he acted like he didn't know who I was.
I called my AAU coach and asked him what was going on. He called the assistants who really wanted me and they said he knows who I am that's just him playing mind games. Well even at 18 I didn't play mind games, let me know what it is so I know how to move.

"Recruiting wise I'll give you this, always go with who loves you."

Like I said my coach wanted me to stay but I wasn't with it. I'm still like that today. I don't go anywhere that I'm not wanted. He sent me to a Juco. At that Juco, they had all little guards. That made me work on my low post game. The low post was easy to do because I had the footwork. But I didn't know that until I started working on it. Because that came easy to me I started working on my turnaround fade away. That came in handy because now I can post up dudes my size or a little bit bigger. This just made me much harder to stop, because now when I was tired I can still score, I'll just go to the low or high post.

For whatever reason, the coach didn't like my game and I didn't care because I didn't like his coaching style. He was another mind playing coach. I know what you're thinking, "All coaches play mind games." Not really, I played for 2 coaches that just said what it is so I'm not used to trying to read minds nor do I like it. The truth may be hard to take but at least people know where they stand. It also leaves them the choice to decide if they feel can play for you or not.

Anyway, when I came home that summer I had no idea what I was going to do. I had no options and honestly, I was ready to quit basketball. I loved the game but the politics of it make you go through times where you think you hate it. What you really hate is that not many people are doing their job in this thing called basketball for the love. I could write a whole book on that but that's another story.

My step dad had a relationship with a division 3 school that was starting a men's team the upcoming year. He kept trying to talk me into it saying that I could go there set all the records, build a resume, and go overseas which I wasn't trying to hear. Like every other kid all I was thinking about was Division 1. School started at the end of August and I was still at home.

My mom was on me every day about doing something with my life. I had no clue on what to do. Whenever she started with that rant I just left out the house. I was a Hooper all my life and didn't know how to operate in the regular world, nor was I ready to yet. So I ended up at the D3 school a week late not even recruited by the coaches but basically walking on (lol).

The first year was hilarious to me. I was playing the 2 and the coach had his "guys." As the season went on I started to be the guy. Other teams knew I was the best player. I could tell by how I was being guarded when conference play started. We didn't win much because we just didn't have a good team. Funny part about college was I was bored. Because of this my coach thought I had a effort problem. I kind of did because it was hard to play every game knowing you're better than everybody. It wasn't many games where I had real competition. Even when we played top 25 teams or teams with D1 transfers I never played against one that was better than me.

That summer I played in the best pro-am in the Philly area, Puregame Men's League. One of my teammates was my man from high school who was trying to get back in school. I told my coaches about him and told them to come see him play. I also told them I was playing the point.

**They responded with, "Really? They got you playing
the point out here?"
I replied, "I played the point all my life except for now
and my senior year of high school."**

That game they loved my man and wanted him to come to
the school. But more importantly I had like 21 and 9 assist
against Division 1 and overseas players. Glad they got to
see that they were looking at my game totally wrong. I still
played the 2 that year, we went to the championship and
lost. I got hurt in the playoffs and didn't fully recover. I re-
sprained my ankle in the chip game and I know we
would've won if I was healthy.

After the season, coach said he didn't know what we were
going to do about the point guard spot next year. Once
again, I had to remind him I'm a natural point and played it
all my life. For me to be the best player in the conference I
was playing out of position (lol). He said he'll try me at the
point in the summer league we were going to play in. I
turned 21 that summer. I'm not bragging or proud of what
I'm about to say but I had a hangover just about every
game day. I wasn't an alcoholic I just went out on
Saturdays and drank since I was old enough too. I was
averaging like 25 and we started 8-0 and a few of those
teams were D2. I finally proved my point.

That season we started 10-0, were getting top 25 votes, and
I was the second leading scorer in D3. I knew that would
change come conference play. At this point I started to
make habits of the things I spoke on in Chapter 3. Things
like playing against coaches, tendencies and adjustments,
and progressions. My last 2 years I saw every type of
defense you can use to slow down somebody down.

Through all of that we won the league chip and got to the NCAA Tourney in just 3 years of existence. I left school as the leading scorer of all time and still hold that record.

The reason that I could be D3 and coach/train top 100 players is because I've dealt with what they are dealing with. I know exactly where the spots are that you need to get to against any defense. As well as the progressions off of that. You may be working out with somebody that played at a higher level than me but they never dealt with defenses the way I have and had to think through it. I was playing below my level so coaches threw their best at me and I still delivered.

Don't fall for the quality of marketing of these trainers look for the quality of development that have to offer. Who's teaching things you need but don't have? Who can explain the game situation f a drill and in a way that you can visualize it? That's what you look for. My story took longer than I expected. Sorry about that, but it was needed to prove my credibility to be of some guidance to you.

Made in the USA
Coppell, TX
25 May 2021

56233585R10046